THE CHANGEMAKER®

Guide to Studying the Bible

Dear Changemaker,

My name is Jennifer Lucy Tyler. I am a wife, Shih-Tzu lover, Bible teacher, coffee connoisseur, bookworm, fashionista and modern missionary. You see, I am intentional about enjoying the simple things in life, but I'm even more passionate about making an eternal impact on a daily basis. This type of purposeful living is what makes life matter and is the reason why I decided to create this journal. It is my hope that you will commit to putting it to use and my objective is that you will gain a better understanding of who God is, what the Gospel truly means, and God's plan for His children.

Over the years, I have developed a heart for you, Changemaker. I can identify with you. Who are the Changemakers? We are the dreamers but we are also the doers. We are the ones who pray and then jump shortly after. Sometimes we are praying as we are jumping. We will jump up and move across the country or even the ocean to pursue a dream. We are the ones protesting for causes we believe in, but we are also the ones organizing and mobilizing. We are the ones who take bold steps of faith to run for office, and we are the ones who decide to teach the next generation in the classroom. We are the women who decide to stay home and homeschool our children and we are also the women climbing the corporate ladder. We are the ones who start businesses and non-profits. We host podcasts and radio shows. We are Influencers and You-Tubers. We are students in a traditional sense but we are also lifetime learners.

Changemaker, if we are honest with ourselves, many of us rarely put in the time to study the Bible. Sure, we use the devotional apps, or we may even listen to a sermon while in the car headed to work. At best, we make it to church on Sunday and try to attend some type of Bible study or small group. Then there are days we finally do make time to spend with God. We get out our favorite Bible, some highlighters, a journal, a cup of coffee in hand, and we get started. Oh but wait, "first let's photograph this cute set up for Instagram because of course, I need to show everyone that I study my Bible." After we edit the perfectly staged photo, we upload and then wait for likes. Is this starting to sound familiar? Since you're on Instagram, you start scrolling, and you see a post that is super interesting. As you begin to read it, your kid begins to knock on your door repeatedly. He or she has a question that must be answered immediately or life as we know it will end. At this point, you have absolutely lost your train of thought and you really don't even know where to begin with your Bible study; so you flip open the Bible to the middle and you land in the book of Amos. You then proceed to read Amos but become distracted because you don't know who Amos is and you start thinking about how you could use some Famous Amos cookies. You head to the kitchen to quickly grab a snack and then back to the room to continue your quiet time; however, your husband has some pressing things to share with you. You're a good wife so you sit and listen to your husband. Before you know it, the hour you had set aside for your personal Bible study is now gone. You sigh with disappointment and just tell yourself that you will make it up tomorrow.

Now, this may sound a bit dramatic, but I am sure there is something in that scenario that we can all relate to. Sometimes "spiritual warfare" comes in the form of distraction. Yes, we war against the Enemy, but sometimes the enemy that we war against is the man or woman in the mirror. Distractions are all around us and as Changemakers, we have the tendency to become consumed by them. My prayer is that this journal will help to guide you during your study time so that you'll know exactly where to start and how to work through the text. This journal, however, will not keep you from the distractions. I can almost promise you that when you sit down with this journal the distractions will attempt to hinder you. That's why the critical first step to take before you begin to study is to pray.

BEFORE YOU START TO USE THIS JOURNAL DURING YOUR STUDY TIME. PLEASE MAKE SURE TO READ THROUGH THE FOLLOWING STEPS:

1. Pray. Hebrews 4:12 says, " For the word of God is living and active, sharper than any two-edged sword, piercing to the division of soul and of spirit, of joints and of marrow, and discerning the thoughts and intentions of the heart." Picture your Bible literally as a sword that you carry as you head off to battle. The word of God has the power to pierce our hearts and transform us. This is why we must never go into studying God's word without prayer. The Enemy knows the power of God's word and this is why he does everything he can to keep us away from it. We also pray because we need the Holy Spirit to be our guide as we work through the text. John 16:13 reminds us that one of the Holy Spirit's roles is to "guide you into all truth." Prayer is the time to invite Him into our study time so that He can reveal truth to us.

2. Read Through the Entire Text or Passage Every Time you Study. I encourage you to read the text out loud with no interruptions. "Faith comes from hearing, and hearing through the word of Christ." (Romans 10:17 English Standard Version) Reading through the entire text multiple times also helps with memorization. Soon you will be able to recall and make connections to other passages of scripture as you study. The Word will be planted in your heart from consistently reading it.

3. Go Back and Highlight or Circle Words that you Do Not Understand and Look Them Up Using a Bible Dictionary and/or Concordance. See our resources guide in the back for suggestions for online dictionaries. Be sure to write out the definitions of words that you don't understand. I love using concordances because I can find out the original Greek and Hebrew meanings of words. For example, did you know that the word "love" has four different Greek meanings in the New Testament? If you don't know which "love" the writer is using, you could get the meaning totally mixed up and interpret the passage incorrectly. So take your time as you circle and highlight words to look up and then write down the definitions. Re-read the passage aloud a second time. I'm sure you're now able to read with an even greater general understanding but hold on, your study time is just beginning!

4. Begin Using Your Changemaker Guide to Studying the Bible. By now, you should have a better understanding of the general message/meaning of the passage. Now that you have prepared for your inductive bible study, you can take out the Changemaker Guide to Studying the Bible and begin to use our worksheets to work through the text. The worksheets provide questions that will help you conduct a thorough exegesis of the passage. Exegesis is simply a critical explanation or interpretation of a text, especially scripture. If I am studying a certain passage, I like to rewrite the passage in my own words. When you can rewrite something in your own words, you know that you have a good comprehensive understanding of the text.

5. Pray throughout your Bible Study Time. If there is a time that you come to a mental block, do not get discouraged. Remember John 16:13, and allow the Holy Spirit to lead and guide you into all truth. This is why prayer is so key during our study time, not just beforehand. You will find that as you pray the Holy Spirit will illuminate His truth to you. It is during these times that I may also consult Bible study notes or commentaries. (See Resources page for suggestions)

6. Don't rush! We often feel the need to rush through the passage. Take your time and stay there. Studying the Bible is not a race; it's not even a marathon. It is a lifelong journey of exploration. There are times when I find myself studying one book of the Bible for several months. I may even remain on one passage or chapter of scripture for several weeks. The time that it takes you to truly study, interpret and comprehend a passage is not what is important. What matters most is that you understand God's Word and that it is getting into your heart and mind.

Inductive Bible Study

WHO IS THE AUTHOR?

_____
_____
_____
_____
_____
_____
_____

WHO ARE THE RECIPIENTS?

_____
_____
_____
_____
_____
_____
_____

IN WHAT STYLE OR GENRE WAS IT WRITTEN?

_____
_____
_____
_____
_____
_____
_____

GENRES OF BIBLICAL LITERATURE

HISTORICAL NARRATIVE/EPIC:

Genesis, Exodus 1-19, Numbers, Joshua, Judges, Ruth, 1 & 2 Samuel, 1 & 2 Kings, 1 & 2 Chronicles, Ezra, Nehemiah, Esther, Jonah, and possibly Acts

THE LAW:

Exodus 20-40, Leviticus, Deuteronomy

WISDOM:

Job, Proverbs, Ecclesiastes

POETRY:

Psalms, Song of Solomon, Lamentations

PROPHECY:

Isaiah, Jeremiah, Ezekiel, Daniel, Hosea, Joel, Amos, Obadiah, Jonah, Micah, Nahum, Habakkuk, Zephaniah, Haggai, Zechariah, Malachi

APOCALYPTIC:

Daniel, Revelation

GOSPEL:

Matthew, Mark, Luke, John, and possibly Acts

EPISTLE (LETTER):

Romans, 1 & 2 Corinthians, Galatians, Ephesians, Philippians, Colossians, 1 & 2 Thessalonians, 1 & 2 Timothy, Titus, Philemon, Hebrews, James, 1 & 2 Peter, 1-3 John, Jude

WHAT IS THE CONTEXT? LOOK FOR THE LOCATION. ORIGINAL AUDIENCE. AND SETTING.

_____

_____

_____

_____

_____

_____

_____

WHAT DOES THE CHAPTER/VERSE MEAN?

_____

_____

_____

_____

_____

_____

_____

_____

WHERE DO WE SEE THE GOSPEL WITHIN THE WHAT WE STUDIED?

_____

_____

_____

_____

_____

_____

_____

Application

WHAT ASPECT OF ~~GOD'S CHARACTER~~ HAS THIS BOOK/CHAPTER SHOWN YOU MORE CLEARLY? WHAT STEPS CAN YOU TAKE TO BETTER LIVE IN LIGHT OF THIS TRUTH?

_____

_____

_____

_____

_____

_____

_____

_____

_____

_____

_____

_____

_____

_____

_____

_____

_____

_____

_____

_____

_____

_____

NOTES/COMMENTARY:

Inductive Bible Study

WHO IS THE AUTHOR?

_____
_____
_____
_____
_____
_____
_____

WHO ARE THE RECIPIENTS?

_____
_____
_____
_____
_____
_____
_____

IN WHAT STYLE OR GENRE WAS IT WRITTEN?

_____
_____
_____
_____
_____
_____
_____

GENRES OF BIBLICAL LITERATURE

HISTORICAL NARRATIVE/EPIC:

Genesis, Exodus 1-19, Numbers, Joshua, Judges, Ruth, 1 & 2 Samuel, 1 & 2 Kings, 1 & 2 Chronicles, Ezra, Nehemiah, Esther, Jonah, and possibly Acts

THE LAW:

Exodus 20-40, Leviticus, Deuteronomy

WISDOM:

Job, Proverbs, Ecclesiastes

POETRY:

Psalms, Song of Solomon, Lamentations

PROPHECY:

Isaiah, Jeremiah, Ezekiel, Daniel, Hosea, Joel, Amos, Obadiah, Jonah, Micah, Nahum, Habakkuk, Zephaniah, Haggai, Zechariah, Malachi

APOCALYPTIC:

Daniel, Revelation

GOSPEL:

Matthew, Mark, Luke, John, and possibly Acts

EPISTLE (LETTER):

Romans, 1 & 2 Corinthians, Galatians, Ephesians, Philippians, Colossians, 1 & 2 Thessalonians, 1 & 2 Timothy, Titus, Philemon, Hebrews, James, 1 & 2 Peter, 1-3 John, Jude

WHAT IS THE CONTEXT? LOOK FOR THE LOCATION. ORIGINAL AUDIENCE.
AND SETTING.

_____

_____

_____

_____

_____

_____

_____

WHAT DOES THE CHAPTER/VERSE MEAN?

_____

_____

_____

_____

_____

_____

_____

_____

WHERE DO WE SEE THE GOSPEL WITHIN THE WHAT WE STUDIED?

_____

_____

_____

_____

_____

_____

_____

Application

WHAT ASPECT OF ~~GOD'S CHARACTER~~ HAS THIS BOOK/CHAPTER SHOWN YOU MORE CLEARLY? WHAT STEPS CAN YOU TAKE TO BETTER LIVE IN LIGHT OF THIS TRUTH?

_____

_____

_____

_____

_____

_____

_____

_____

_____

_____

_____

_____

_____

_____

_____

_____

_____

_____

_____

_____

_____

_____

NOTES/COMMENTARY:

 Inductive Bible Study

WHO IS THE AUTHOR?

_____
_____
_____
_____
_____
_____
_____

WHO ARE THE RECIPIENTS?

_____
_____
_____
_____
_____
_____
_____

IN WHAT STYLE OR GENRE WAS IT WRITTEN?

_____
_____
_____
_____
_____
_____
_____

GENRES OF BIBLICAL LITERATURE

HISTORICAL NARRATIVE/EPIC:

Genesis, Exodus 1-19, Numbers, Joshua, Judges, Ruth, 1 & 2 Samuel, 1 & 2 Kings, 1 & 2 Chronicles, Ezra, Nehemiah, Esther, Jonah, and possibly Acts

THE LAW:

Exodus 20-40, Leviticus, Deuteronomy

WISDOM:

Job, Proverbs, Ecclesiastes

POETRY:

Psalms, Song of Solomon, Lamentations

PROPHECY:

Isaiah, Jeremiah, Ezekiel, Daniel, Hosea, Joel, Amos, Obadiah, Jonah, Micah, Nahum, Habakkuk, Zephaniah, Haggai, Zechariah, Malachi

APOCALYPTIC:

Daniel, Revelation

GOSPEL:

Matthew, Mark, Luke, John, and possibly Acts

EPISTLE (LETTER):

Romans, 1 & 2 Corinthians, Galatians, Ephesians, Philippians, Colossians, 1 & 2 Thessalonians, 1 & 2 Timothy, Titus, Philemon, Hebrews, James, 1 & 2 Peter, 1-3 John, Jude

WHAT IS THE CONTEXT? LOOK FOR THE LOCATION. ORIGINAL AUDIENCE.
AND SETTING.

_____
_____
_____
_____
_____
_____
_____

WHAT DOES THE CHAPTER/VERSE MEAN?

_____
_____
_____
_____
_____
_____
_____
_____

WHERE DO WE SEE THE GOSPEL WITHIN THE WHAT WE STUDIED?

_____
_____
_____
_____
_____
_____
_____

Application

WHAT ASPECT OF ~~GOD'S CHARACTER~~ HAS THIS BOOK/CHAPTER SHOWN YOU MORE CLEARLY? WHAT STEPS CAN YOU TAKE TO BETTER LIVE IN LIGHT OF THIS TRUTH?

_____

_____

_____

_____

_____

_____

_____

_____

_____

_____

_____

_____

_____

_____

_____

_____

_____

_____

_____

_____

_____

_____

_____

_____

NOTES/COMMENTARY:

 *Inductive Bible Study*

WHO IS THE AUTHOR?

_____

_____

_____

_____

_____

_____

_____

WHO ARE THE RECIPIENTS?

_____

_____

_____

_____

_____

_____

_____

IN WHAT STYLE OR GENRE WAS IT WRITTEN?

_____

_____

_____

_____

_____

_____

GENRES OF BIBLICAL LITERATURE

HISTORICAL NARRATIVE/EPIC:

Genesis, Exodus 1-19, Numbers, Joshua, Judges, Ruth, 1 & 2 Samuel, 1 & 2 Kings, 1 & 2 Chronicles, Ezra, Nehemiah, Esther, Jonah, and possibly Acts

THE LAW:

Exodus 20-40, Leviticus, Deuteronomy

WISDOM:

Job, Proverbs, Ecclesiastes

POETRY:

Psalms, Song of Solomon, Lamentations

PROPHECY:

Isaiah, Jeremiah, Ezekiel, Daniel, Hosea, Joel, Amos, Obadiah, Jonah, Micah, Nahum, Habakkuk, Zephaniah, Haggai, Zechariah, Malachi

APOCALYPTIC:

Daniel, Revelation

GOSPEL:

Matthew, Mark, Luke, John, and possibly Acts

EPISTLE (LETTER):

Romans, 1 & 2 Corinthians, Galatians, Ephesians, Philippians, Colossians, 1 & 2 Thessalonians, 1 & 2 Timothy, Titus, Philemon, Hebrews, James, 1 & 2 Peter, 1-3 John, Jude

WHAT IS THE CONTEXT? LOOK FOR THE LOCATION, ORIGINAL AUDIENCE, AND SETTING.

_____

_____

_____

_____

_____

_____

_____

WHAT DOES THE CHAPTER/VERSE MEAN?

_____

_____

_____

_____

_____

_____

_____

WHERE DO WE SEE THE GOSPEL WITHIN THE WHAT WE STUDIED?

_____

_____

_____

_____

_____

_____

Application

WHAT ASPECT OF ~~GOD'S CHARACTER~~ HAS THIS BOOK/CHAPTER SHOWN YOU MORE CLEARLY? WHAT STEPS CAN YOU TAKE TO BETTER LIVE IN LIGHT OF THIS TRUTH?

_____

_____

_____

_____

_____

_____

_____

_____

_____

_____

_____

_____

_____

_____

_____

_____

_____

_____

_____

_____

_____

_____

_____

NOTES/COMMENTARY:

Inductive Bible Study

WHO IS THE AUTHOR?

_____
_____
_____
_____
_____
_____
_____

WHO ARE THE RECIPIENTS?

_____
_____
_____
_____
_____
_____

IN WHAT STYLE OR GENRE WAS IT WRITTEN?

_____
_____
_____
_____
_____
_____
_____

GENRES OF BIBLICAL LITERATURE

HISTORICAL NARRATIVE/EPIC:

Genesis, Exodus 1-19, Numbers, Joshua, Judges, Ruth, 1 & 2 Samuel, 1 & 2 Kings, 1 & 2 Chronicles, Ezra, Nehemiah, Esther, Jonah, and possibly Acts

THE LAW:

Exodus 20-40, Leviticus, Deuteronomy

WISDOM:

Job, Proverbs, Ecclesiastes

POETRY:

Psalms, Song of Solomon, Lamentations

PROPHECY:

Isaiah, Jeremiah, Ezekiel, Daniel, Hosea, Joel, Amos, Obadiah, Jonah, Micah, Nahum, Habakkuk, Zephaniah, Haggai, Zechariah, Malachi

APOCALYPTIC:

Daniel, Revelation

GOSPEL:

Matthew, Mark, Luke, John, and possibly Acts

EPISTLE (LETTER):

Romans, 1 & 2 Corinthians, Galatians, Ephesians, Philippians, Colossians, 1 & 2 Thessalonians, 1 & 2 Timothy, Titus, Philemon, Hebrews, James, 1 & 2 Peter, 1-3 John, Jude

WHAT IS THE CONTEXT? LOOK FOR THE LOCATION. ORIGINAL AUDIENCE. AND SETTING.

_____

_____

_____

_____

_____

_____

_____

WHAT DOES THE CHAPTER/VERSE MEAN?

_____

_____

_____

_____

_____

_____

_____

_____

WHERE DO WE SEE THE GOSPEL WITHIN THE WHAT WE STUDIED?

_____

_____

_____

_____

_____

_____

_____

Application

WHAT ASPECT OF ~~GOD'S CHARACTER~~ HAS THIS BOOK/CHAPTER SHOWN YOU MORE CLEARLY? WHAT STEPS CAN YOU TAKE TO BETTER LIVE IN LIGHT OF THIS TRUTH?

_____

_____

_____

_____

_____

_____

_____

_____

_____

_____

_____

_____

_____

_____

_____

_____

_____

_____

_____

_____

_____

NOTES/COMMENTARY:

Inductive Bible Study

WHO IS THE AUTHOR?

_____

_____

_____

_____

_____

_____

_____

WHO ARE THE RECIPIENTS?

_____

_____

_____

_____

_____

_____

_____

IN WHAT STYLE OR GENRE WAS IT WRITTEN?

_____

_____

_____

_____

_____

_____

_____

GENRES OF BIBLICAL LITERATURE

HISTORICAL NARRATIVE/EPIC:

Genesis, Exodus 1-19, Numbers, Joshua, Judges, Ruth, 1 & 2 Samuel, 1 & 2 Kings, 1 & 2 Chronicles, Ezra, Nehemiah, Esther, Jonah, and possibly Acts

THE LAW:

Exodus 20-40, Leviticus, Deuteronomy

WISDOM:

Job, Proverbs, Ecclesiastes

POETRY:

Psalms, Song of Solomon, Lamentations

PROPHECY:

Isaiah, Jeremiah, Ezekiel, Daniel, Hosea, Joel, Amos, Obadiah, Jonah, Micah, Nahum, Habakkuk, Zephaniah, Haggai, Zechariah, Malachi

APOCALYPTIC:

Daniel, Revelation

GOSPEL:

Matthew, Mark, Luke, John, and possibly Acts

EPISTLE (LETTER):

Romans, 1 & 2 Corinthians, Galatians, Ephesians, Philippians, Colossians, 1 & 2 Thessalonians, 1 & 2 Timothy, Titus, Philemon, Hebrews, James, 1 & 2 Peter, 1-3 John, Jude

WHAT IS THE CONTEXT? LOOK FOR THE LOCATION, ORIGINAL AUDIENCE, AND SETTING.

_____
_____
_____
_____
_____
_____
_____

WHAT DOES THE CHAPTER/VERSE MEAN?

_____
_____
_____
_____
_____
_____
_____
_____

WHERE DO WE SEE THE GOSPEL WITHIN THE WHAT WE STUDIED?

_____
_____
_____
_____
_____
_____
_____

Application

WHAT ASPECT OF ~~GOD'S CHARACTER~~ HAS THIS BOOK/CHAPTER SHOWN YOU MORE CLEARLY? WHAT STEPS CAN YOU TAKE TO BETTER LIVE IN LIGHT OF THIS TRUTH?

_____

_____

_____

_____

_____

_____

_____

_____

_____

_____

_____

_____

_____

_____

_____

_____

_____

_____

_____

_____

_____

_____

NOTES/COMMENTARY:

 *Inductive Bible Study*

WHO IS THE AUTHOR?

_____
_____
_____
_____
_____
_____
_____

WHO ARE THE RECIPIENTS?

_____
_____
_____
_____
_____
_____
_____

IN WHAT STYLE OR GENRE WAS IT WRITTEN?

_____
_____
_____
_____
_____
_____
_____

GENRES OF BIBLICAL LITERATURE

HISTORICAL NARRATIVE/EPIC:

Genesis, Exodus 1-19, Numbers, Joshua, Judges, Ruth, 1 & 2 Samuel, 1 & 2 Kings, 1 & 2 Chronicles, Ezra, Nehemiah, Esther, Jonah, and possibly Acts

THE LAW:

Exodus 20-40, Leviticus, Deuteronomy

WISDOM:

Job, Proverbs, Ecclesiastes

POETRY:

Psalms, Song of Solomon, Lamentations

PROPHECY:

Isaiah, Jeremiah, Ezekiel, Daniel, Hosea, Joel, Amos, Obadiah, Jonah, Micah, Nahum, Habakkuk, Zephaniah, Haggai, Zechariah, Malachi

APOCALYPTIC:

Daniel, Revelation

GOSPEL:

Matthew, Mark, Luke, John, and possibly Acts

EPISTLE (LETTER):

Romans, 1 & 2 Corinthians, Galatians, Ephesians, Philippians, Colossians, 1 & 2 Thessalonians, 1 & 2 Timothy, Titus, Philemon, Hebrews, James, 1 & 2 Peter, 1-3 John, Jude

WHAT IS THE CONTEXT? LOOK FOR THE LOCATION, ORIGINAL AUDIENCE, AND SETTING.

_____

_____

_____

_____

_____

_____

WHAT DOES THE CHAPTER/VERSE MEAN?

_____

_____

_____

_____

_____

_____

_____

WHERE DO WE SEE THE GOSPEL WITHIN THE WHAT WE STUDIED?

_____

_____

_____

_____

_____

_____

_____

Application

WHAT ASPECT OF ~~GOD'S CHARACTER~~ HAS THIS BOOK/CHAPTER SHOWN YOU MORE CLEARLY? WHAT STEPS CAN YOU TAKE TO BETTER LIVE IN LIGHT OF THIS TRUTH?

_____

_____

_____

_____

_____

_____

_____

_____

_____

_____

_____

_____

_____

_____

_____

_____

_____

_____

_____

_____

_____

_____

NOTES/COMMENTARY:

WHO IS THE AUTHOR?

_____
_____
_____
_____
_____
_____
_____
_____

WHO ARE THE RECIPIENTS?

_____
_____
_____
_____
_____
_____
_____

IN WHAT STYLE OR GENRE WAS IT WRITTEN?

_____
_____
_____
_____
_____
_____

GENRES OF BIBLICAL LITERATURE

HISTORICAL NARRATIVE/EPIC:

Genesis, Exodus 1-19, Numbers, Joshua, Judges, Ruth, 1 & 2 Samuel, 1 & 2 Kings, 1 & 2 Chronicles, Ezra, Nehemiah, Esther, Jonah, and possibly Acts

THE LAW:

Exodus 20-40, Leviticus, Deuteronomy

WISDOM:

Job, Proverbs, Ecclesiastes

POETRY:

Psalms, Song of Solomon, Lamentations

PROPHECY:

Isaiah, Jeremiah, Ezekiel, Daniel, Hosea, Joel, Amos, Obadiah, Jonah, Micah, Nahum, Habakkuk, Zephaniah, Haggai, Zechariah, Malachi

APOCALYPTIC:

Daniel, Revelation

GOSPEL:

Matthew, Mark, Luke, John, and possibly Acts

EPISTLE (LETTER):

Romans, 1 & 2 Corinthians, Galatians, Ephesians, Philippians, Colossians, 1 & 2 Thessalonians, 1 & 2 Timothy, Titus, Philemon, Hebrews, James, 1 & 2 Peter, 1-3 John, Jude

WHAT IS THE CONTEXT? LOOK FOR THE LOCATION. ORIGINAL AUDIENCE.
AND SETTING.

_____

_____

_____

_____

_____

_____

_____

WHAT DOES THE CHAPTER/VERSE MEAN?

_____

_____

_____

_____

_____

_____

_____

_____

WHERE DO WE SEE THE GOSPEL WITHIN THE WHAT WE STUDIED?

_____

_____

_____

_____

_____

_____

_____

_____

Application

WHAT ASPECT OF ~~GOD'S CHARACTER~~ HAS THIS BOOK/CHAPTER SHOWN YOU MORE CLEARLY? WHAT STEPS CAN YOU TAKE TO BETTER LIVE IN LIGHT OF THIS TRUTH?

_____

_____

_____

_____

_____

_____

_____

_____

_____

_____

_____

_____

_____

_____

_____

_____

_____

_____

_____

_____

_____

NOTES/COMMENTARY:

WHO IS THE AUTHOR?

_____
_____
_____
_____
_____
_____
_____

WHO ARE THE RECIPIENTS?

_____
_____
_____
_____
_____
_____
_____

IN WHAT STYLE OR GENRE WAS IT WRITTEN?

_____
_____
_____
_____
_____
_____
_____

GENRES OF BIBLICAL LITERATURE

HISTORICAL NARRATIVE/EPIC:

Genesis, Exodus 1-19, Numbers, Joshua, Judges, Ruth, 1 & 2 Samuel, 1 & 2 Kings, 1 & 2 Chronicles, Ezra, Nehemiah, Esther, Jonah, and possibly Acts

THE LAW:

Exodus 20-40, Leviticus, Deuteronomy

WISDOM:

Job, Proverbs, Ecclesiastes

POETRY:

Psalms, Song of Solomon, Lamentations

PROPHECY:

Isaiah, Jeremiah, Ezekiel, Daniel, Hosea, Joel, Amos, Obadiah, Jonah, Micah, Nahum, Habakkuk, Zephaniah, Haggai, Zechariah, Malachi

APOCALYPTIC:

Daniel, Revelation

GOSPEL:

Matthew, Mark, Luke, John, and possibly Acts

EPISTLE (LETTER):

Romans, 1 & 2 Corinthians, Galatians, Ephesians, Philippians, Colossians, 1 & 2 Thessalonians, 1 & 2 Timothy, Titus, Philemon, Hebrews, James, 1 & 2 Peter, 1-3 John, Jude

WHAT IS THE CONTEXT? LOOK FOR THE LOCATION, ORIGINAL AUDIENCE, AND SETTING.

_____

_____

_____

_____

_____

_____

_____

WHAT DOES THE CHAPTER/VERSE MEAN?

_____

_____

_____

_____

_____

_____

_____

_____

_____

WHERE DO WE SEE THE GOSPEL WITHIN THE WHAT WE STUDIED?

_____

_____

_____

_____

_____

_____

_____

Application

WHAT ASPECT OF ~~GOD'S CHARACTER~~ HAS THIS BOOK/CHAPTER SHOWN YOU MORE CLEARLY? WHAT STEPS CAN YOU TAKE TO BETTER LIVE IN LIGHT OF THIS TRUTH?

_____
_____
_____
_____
_____
_____
_____
_____
_____
_____
_____
_____
_____
_____
_____
_____
_____
_____
_____
_____
_____
_____

NOTES/COMMENTARY:

Inductive Bible Study

WHO IS THE AUTHOR?

_____
_____
_____
_____
_____
_____
_____
_____

WHO ARE THE RECIPIENTS?

_____
_____
_____
_____
_____
_____
_____
_____

IN WHAT STYLE OR GENRE WAS IT WRITTEN?

_____
_____
_____
_____
_____
_____
_____

GENRES OF BIBLICAL LITERATURE

HISTORICAL NARRATIVE/EPIC:

Genesis, Exodus 1-19, Numbers, Joshua, Judges, Ruth, 1 & 2 Samuel, 1 & 2 Kings, 1 & 2 Chronicles, Ezra, Nehemiah, Esther, Jonah, and possibly Acts

THE LAW:

Exodus 20-40, Leviticus, Deuteronomy

WISDOM:

Job, Proverbs, Ecclesiastes

POETRY:

Psalms, Song of Solomon, Lamentations

PROPHECY:

Isaiah, Jeremiah, Ezekiel, Daniel, Hosea, Joel, Amos, Obadiah, Jonah, Micah, Nahum, Habakkuk, Zephaniah, Haggai, Zechariah, Malachi

APOCALYPTIC:

Daniel, Revelation

GOSPEL:

Matthew, Mark, Luke, John, and possibly Acts

EPISTLE (LETTER):

Romans, 1 & 2 Corinthians, Galatians, Ephesians, Philippians, Colossians, 1 & 2 Thessalonians, 1 & 2 Timothy, Titus, Philemon, Hebrews, James, 1 & 2 Peter, 1-3 John, Jude

WHAT IS THE CONTEXT? LOOK FOR THE LOCATION. ORIGINAL AUDIENCE.
AND SETTING.

_____

_____

_____

_____

_____

_____

_____

WHAT DOES THE CHAPTER/VERSE MEAN?

_____

_____

_____

_____

_____

_____

_____

_____

WHERE DO WE SEE THE GOSPEL WITHIN THE WHAT WE STUDIED?

_____

_____

_____

_____

_____

_____

_____

Application

WHAT ASPECT OF ~~GOD'S CHARACTER~~ HAS THIS BOOK/CHAPTER SHOWN YOU MORE CLEARLY? WHAT STEPS CAN YOU TAKE TO BETTER LIVE IN LIGHT OF THIS TRUTH?

_____

_____

_____

_____

_____

_____

_____

_____

_____

_____

_____

_____

_____

_____

_____

_____

_____

_____

_____

_____

_____

_____

NOTES/COMMENTARY:

 *Inductive Bible Study*

WHO IS THE AUTHOR?

_____
_____
_____
_____
_____
_____
_____

WHO ARE THE RECIPIENTS?

_____
_____
_____
_____
_____
_____

IN WHAT STYLE OR GENRE WAS IT WRITTEN?

_____
_____
_____
_____
_____
_____

GENRES OF BIBLICAL LITERATURE

HISTORICAL NARRATIVE/EPIC:

Genesis, Exodus 1-19, Numbers, Joshua, Judges, Ruth, 1 & 2 Samuel, 1 & 2 Kings, 1 & 2 Chronicles, Ezra, Nehemiah, Esther, Jonah, and possibly Acts

THE LAW:

Exodus 20-40, Leviticus, Deuteronomy

WISDOM:

Job, Proverbs, Ecclesiastes

POETRY:

Psalms, Song of Solomon, Lamentations

PROPHECY:

Isaiah, Jeremiah, Ezekiel, Daniel, Hosea, Joel, Amos, Obadiah, Jonah, Micah, Nahum, Habakkuk, Zephaniah, Haggai, Zechariah, Malachi

APOCALYPTIC:

Daniel, Revelation

GOSPEL:

Matthew, Mark, Luke, John, and possibly Acts

EPISTLE (LETTER):

Romans, 1 & 2 Corinthians, Galatians, Ephesians, Philippians, Colossians, 1 & 2 Thessalonians, 1 & 2 Timothy, Titus, Philemon, Hebrews, James, 1 & 2 Peter, 1-3 John, Jude

WHAT IS THE CONTEXT? LOOK FOR THE LOCATION. ORIGINAL AUDIENCE. AND SETTING.

_____

_____

_____

_____

_____

_____

_____

WHAT DOES THE CHAPTER/VERSE MEAN?

_____

_____

_____

_____

_____

_____

_____

_____

WHERE DO WE SEE THE GOSPEL WITHIN THE WHAT WE STUDIED?

_____

_____

_____

_____

_____

_____

_____

Application

WHAT ASPECT OF ~~GOD'S CHARACTER~~ HAS THIS BOOK/CHAPTER SHOWN YOU MORE CLEARLY? WHAT STEPS CAN YOU TAKE TO BETTER LIVE IN LIGHT OF THIS TRUTH?

_____

_____

_____

_____

_____

_____

_____

_____

_____

_____

_____

_____

_____

_____

_____

_____

_____

_____

_____

_____

_____

_____

_____

NOTES/COMMENTARY:

Inductive Bible Study

WHO IS THE AUTHOR?

_____

_____

_____

_____

_____

_____

WHO ARE THE RECIPIENTS?

_____

_____

_____

_____

_____

_____

IN WHAT STYLE OR GENRE WAS IT WRITTEN?

_____

_____

_____

_____

_____

_____

GENRES OF BIBLICAL LITERATURE

HISTORICAL NARRATIVE/EPIC:

Genesis, Exodus 1-19, Numbers, Joshua, Judges, Ruth, 1 & 2 Samuel, 1 & 2 Kings, 1 & 2 Chronicles, Ezra, Nehemiah, Esther, Jonah, and possibly Acts

THE LAW:

Exodus 20-40, Leviticus, Deuteronomy

WISDOM:

Job, Proverbs, Ecclesiastes

POETRY:

Psalms, Song of Solomon, Lamentations

PROPHECY:

Isaiah, Jeremiah, Ezekiel, Daniel, Hosea, Joel, Amos, Obadiah, Jonah, Micah, Nahum, Habakkuk, Zephaniah, Haggai, Zechariah, Malachi

APOCALYPTIC:

Daniel, Revelation

GOSPEL:

Matthew, Mark, Luke, John, and possibly Acts

EPISTLE (LETTER):

Romans, 1 & 2 Corinthians, Galatians, Ephesians, Philippians, Colossians, 1 & 2 Thessalonians, 1 & 2 Timothy, Titus, Philemon, Hebrews, James, 1 & 2 Peter, 1-3 John, Jude

WHAT IS THE CONTEXT? LOOK FOR THE LOCATION. ORIGINAL AUDIENCE. AND SETTING.

_____
_____
_____
_____
_____
_____
_____
_____

WHAT DOES THE CHAPTER/VERSE MEAN?

_____
_____
_____
_____
_____
_____
_____
_____
_____

WHERE DO WE SEE THE GOSPEL WITHIN THE WHAT WE STUDIED?

_____
_____
_____
_____
_____
_____
_____
_____

Application

WHAT ASPECT OF ~~GOD'S CHARACTER~~ HAS THIS BOOK/CHAPTER SHOWN YOU MORE CLEARLY? WHAT STEPS CAN YOU TAKE TO BETTER LIVE IN LIGHT OF THIS TRUTH?

_____

_____

_____

_____

_____

_____

_____

_____

_____

_____

_____

_____

_____

_____

_____

_____

_____

_____

_____

_____

_____

_____

_____

NOTES/COMMENTARY:

THE CHARACTER OF GOD

○ _____
○ _____
○ _____
○ _____
○ _____
○ _____
○ _____
○ _____
○ _____
○ _____

THE PROMISES OF GOD

○ _____
○ _____
○ _____
○ _____
○ _____
○ _____
○ _____
○ _____
○ _____
○ _____

PRAYERS FOR LOVED ONES

○ _____
○ _____
○ _____
○ _____
○ _____
○ _____
○ _____
○ _____
○ _____
○ _____

PRAYERS REQUESTS FROM OTHERS

○ _____
○ _____
○ _____
○ _____
○ _____
○ _____
○ _____
○ _____
○ _____
○ _____

prayer journal

THE CHARACTER OF GOD

○ _____
○ _____
○ _____
○ _____
○ _____
○ _____
○ _____
○ _____
○ _____
○ _____

THE PROMISES OF GOD

○ _____
○ _____
○ _____
○ _____
○ _____
○ _____
○ _____
○ _____
○ _____
○ _____

PRAYERS FOR LOVED ONES

○ _____
○ _____
○ _____
○ _____
○ _____
○ _____
○ _____
○ _____
○ _____
○ _____

PRAYERS REQUESTS FROM OTHERS

○ _____
○ _____
○ _____
○ _____
○ _____
○ _____
○ _____
○ _____
○ _____
○ _____

prayer journal

THE CHARACTER OF GOD

- ○ _____
- ○ _____
- ○ _____
- ○ _____
- ○ _____
- ○ _____
- ○ _____
- ○ _____
- ○ _____
- ○ _____

THE PROMISES OF GOD

- ○ _____
- ○ _____
- ○ _____
- ○ _____
- ○ _____
- ○ _____
- ○ _____
- ○ _____
- ○ _____
- ○ _____

PRAYERS FOR LOVED ONES

- ○ _____
- ○ _____
- ○ _____
- ○ _____
- ○ _____
- ○ _____
- ○ _____
- ○ _____
- ○ _____
- ○ _____

PRAYERS REQUESTS FROM OTHERS

- ○ _____
- ○ _____
- ○ _____
- ○ _____
- ○ _____
- ○ _____
- ○ _____
- ○ _____
- ○ _____
- ○ _____

prayer journal

THE CHARACTER OF GOD

- ○ _____
- ○ _____
- ○ _____
- ○ _____
- ○ _____
- ○ _____
- ○ _____
- ○ _____
- ○ _____
- ○ _____

THE PROMISES OF GOD

- ○ _____
- ○ _____
- ○ _____
- ○ _____
- ○ _____
- ○ _____
- ○ _____
- ○ _____
- ○ _____
- ○ _____

PRAYERS FOR LOVED ONES

- ○ _____
- ○ _____
- ○ _____
- ○ _____
- ○ _____
- ○ _____
- ○ _____
- ○ _____
- ○ _____
- ○ _____

PRAYERS REQUESTS FROM OTHERS

- ○ _____
- ○ _____
- ○ _____
- ○ _____
- ○ _____
- ○ _____
- ○ _____
- ○ _____
- ○ _____
- ○ _____

 prayer journal

THE CHARACTER OF GOD

○ _____
○ _____
○ _____
○ _____
○ _____
○ _____
○ _____
○ _____
○ _____
○ _____

THE PROMISES OF GOD

○ _____
○ _____
○ _____
○ _____
○ _____
○ _____
○ _____
○ _____
○ _____
○ _____

PRAYERS FOR LOVED ONES

○ _____
○ _____
○ _____
○ _____
○ _____
○ _____
○ _____
○ _____
○ _____
○ _____

PRAYERS REQUESTS FROM OTHERS

○ _____
○ _____
○ _____
○ _____
○ _____
○ _____
○ _____
○ _____
○ _____
○ _____

THE CHARACTER OF GOD

- _____
- _____
- _____
- _____
- _____
- _____
- _____
- _____
- _____
- _____

THE PROMISES OF GOD

- _____
- _____
- _____
- _____
- _____
- _____
- _____
- _____
- _____
- _____

PRAYERS FOR LOVED ONES

- _____
- _____
- _____
- _____
- _____
- _____
- _____
- _____
- _____
- _____

PRAYERS REQUESTS FROM OTHERS

- _____
- _____
- _____
- _____
- _____
- _____
- _____
- _____
- _____
- _____

 prayer journal

THE CHARACTER OF GOD

○ _____
○ _____
○ _____
○ _____
○ _____
○ _____
○ _____
○ _____
○ _____
○ _____

THE PROMISES OF GOD

○ _____
○ _____
○ _____
○ _____
○ _____
○ _____
○ _____
○ _____
○ _____
○ _____

PRAYERS FOR LOVED ONES

○ _____
○ _____
○ _____
○ _____
○ _____
○ _____
○ _____
○ _____
○ _____
○ _____

PRAYERS REQUESTS FROM OTHERS

○ _____
○ _____
○ _____
○ _____
○ _____
○ _____
○ _____
○ _____
○ _____
○ _____

Scripture Memorization

First we will Read the passage 10 times, and then say the passage aloud 10 times.

WITHOUT LOOKING IN YOUR BIBLE. FILL OUT THE MISSING VERSES TO ROMANS 8:28-29. USE YOUR MEMORY ONLY. (WE USED THE ESV TRANSLATION)

And we _know_ that for those who _love_ God all things work together _for good_, for those who are _called_ according to his _purpose_. For _those whom_ he foreknew he also _predestined_ to be conformed _to the image_ of his Son, in order that he _might_ be the _firstborn among_ many brothers.

WRITE OUT ROMANS 8:28-29

And we know that for those who love God all things work together for good, for those who are called according to his purpose. For those whom he foreknew, he also predestined to be conformed to the image of his Son, in order that he might be the firstborn among many brothers.

ANOTHER UNIQUE WAY TO MEMORIZE SCRIPTURE IS TO WRITE ONLY THE FIRST LETTER OF EACH WORD. TRY IT BELOW USING ROMANS 8:28. (SEPARATE) EACH LETTER WITH A COMMA)

A, W, K, T, F, T, W, L, G, A, T, W, T, F, G, F, T, W, A, C,
A, T, H, P.

Scripture Memorization

First we will Read the passage 10 times, and then say the passage aloud 10 times.

WITHOUT LOOKING IN YOUR BIBLE. FILL OUT THE MISSING VERSES TO PSALM 115:3. USE YOUR MEMORY ONLY. (WE USED THE ESV TRANSLATION)

Our God is in _____ _____; he _____ ____ _____ he pleases.

WRITE OUT PSALM 115:3

_____

_____

_____

_____

_____

_____

ANOTHER UNIQUE WAY TO MEMORIZE SCRIPTURE IS TO WRITE ONLY THE FIRST LETTER OF EACH WORD. TRY IT BELOW USING THIS PASSAGE. (SEPARATE) EACH LETTER WITH A COMMA)

_____

_____

_____

_____

Scripture Memorization

First we will Read the passage 10 times, and then say the passage aloud 10 times.

WITHOUT LOOKING IN YOUR BIBLE. FILL OUT THE MISSING VERSES TO JUDE 1:24-25. USE YOUR MEMORY ONLY. (WE USED THE ESV TRANSLATION)

Now to him who ____ _____ to keep you from stumbling and ____ _____ you blameless before the _____ ____ _____ glory with great joy, to ____ _____ _____, our Savior, _____ Jesus Christ our Lord, ____ _____, majesty, _____, and authority, before all time and _____ ____ _____. Amen.

WRITE OUT JUDE 1:24-25

_____
_____
_____
_____
_____
_____
_____

ANOTHER UNIQUE WAY TO MEMORIZE SCRIPTURE IS TO WRITE ONLY THE FIRST LETTER OF EACH WORD. TRY IT BELOW USING THIS PASSAGE. (SEPARATE) EACH LETTER WITH A COMMA)

_____
_____
_____
_____

First we will Read the passage 10 times, and then say the passage aloud 10 times.

WITHOUT LOOKING IN YOUR BIBLE. FILL OUT THE MISSING VERSES TO 1 JOHN 2:29. USE YOUR MEMORY ONLY. (WE USED THE ESV TRANSLATION)

If you know that ___ ___ _____, you may be sure that _____ ____ practices righteousness has _____ _____ of him.

WRITE OUT 1 JOHN 2:29

_____

_____

_____

_____

_____

_____

_____

ANOTHER UNIQUE WAY TO MEMORIZE SCRIPTURE IS TO WRITE ONLY THE FIRST LETTER OF EACH WORD. TRY IT BELOW USING THIS PASSAGE. (SEPARATE) EACH LETTER WITH A COMMA)

_____

_____

_____

_____

First we will Read the passage 10 times, and then say the passage aloud 10 times.

WITHOUT LOOKING IN YOUR BIBLE. FILL OUT THE MISSING VERSES TO 1 CORINTHIANS 1:30-31. USE YOUR MEMORY ONLY. (WE USED THE ESV TRANSLATION)

And _____ _____ _____ you are in Christ Jesus, who _____ to us wisdom from God, righteousness and _____ and redemption, so that, as ____ ____ _____, "Let the one who boasts, _____ ____ the Lord."

WRITE OUT 1 CORINTHIANS 1:30-31

_____

_____

_____

_____

_____

_____

_____

ANOTHER UNIQUE WAY TO MEMORIZE SCRIPTURE IS TO WRITE ONLY THE FIRST LETTER OF EACH WORD. TRY IT BELOW USING THIS PASSAGE. (SEPARATE) EACH LETTER WITH A COMMA)

_____

_____

_____

_____

Scripture Memorization

First we will Read the passage 10 times, and then say the passage aloud 10 times.

WITHOUT LOOKING IN YOUR BIBLE. FILL OUT THE MISSING VERSES TO JOHN 15:16. USE YOUR MEMORY ONLY. (WE USED THE ESV TRANSLATION)

You did not _____ ____, but I chose you and _____ _____ that you should go and _____ _____ and that your fruit should _____, so that whatever you _____ _____ _____ in my name, he may _____ ____ to you.

WRITE OUT JOHN 15:16

_____

_____

_____

_____

_____

_____

_____

ANOTHER UNIQUE WAY TO MEMORIZE SCRIPTURE IS TO WRITE ONLY THE FIRST LETTER OF EACH WORD. TRY IT BELOW USING THIS PASSAGE. (SEPARATE) EACH LETTER WITH A COMMA)

_____

_____

_____

_____

Scripture Memorization

First we will Read the passage 10 times, and then say the passage aloud 10 times.

WITHOUT LOOKING IN YOUR BIBLE. FILL OUT THE MISSING VERSES TO PHILIPPIANS 1:6. USE YOUR MEMORY ONLY. (WE USED THE ESV TRANSLATION)

And I am _____ _____ this, that he who _____ ____ _____ work in you will bring it ____ _____ at the day of _____ _____.

WRITE OUT PHILIPPIANS 1:6

_____

_____

_____

_____

_____

_____

_____

ANOTHER UNIQUE WAY TO MEMORIZE SCRIPTURE IS TO WRITE ONLY THE FIRST LETTER OF EACH WORD. TRY IT BELOW USING THIS PASSAGE. (SEPARATE) EACH LETTER WITH A COMMA)

_____

_____

_____

_____

First we will Read the passage 10 times, and then say the passage aloud 10 times.

WITHOUT LOOKING IN YOUR BIBLE, FILL OUT THE MISSING VERSES TO JEREMIAH 32:40. USE YOUR MEMORY ONLY. (WE USED THE ESV TRANSLATION)

I will _____ _____ them an everlasting _____, that I will not turn away _____ _____ good to them. And I will _____ _____ _____ of me in their _____, that they may not _____ _____ me.

WRITE OUT JEREMIAH 32:40

_____

_____

_____

_____

_____

_____

ANOTHER UNIQUE WAY TO MEMORIZE SCRIPTURE IS TO WRITE ONLY THE FIRST LETTER OF EACH WORD. TRY IT BELOW USING THIS PASSAGE. (SEPARATE) EACH LETTER WITH A COMMA)

_____

_____

_____

_____

Scripture Memorization

First we will Read the passage 10 times, and then say the passage aloud 10 times.

WITHOUT LOOKING IN YOUR BIBLE, FILL OUT THE MISSING VERSES TO DEUTERONOMY 30:6. USE YOUR MEMORY ONLY. (WE USED THE ESV TRANSLATION)

And the _____ _____ _____ will circumcise your heart and the heart of _____ _____, so that you will _____ the Lord your God with all _____ _____ and with all _____ _____, that you may live.

WRITE OUT DEUTERONOMY 30:6

_____

_____

_____

_____

_____

_____

_____

ANOTHER UNIQUE WAY TO MEMORIZE SCRIPTURE IS TO WRITE ONLY THE FIRST LETTER OF EACH WORD. TRY IT BELOW USING THIS PASSAGE. (SEPARATE) EACH LETTER WITH A COMMA)

_____

_____

_____

_____

First we will Read the passage 10 times, and then say the passage aloud 10 times.

WITHOUT LOOKING IN YOUR BIBLE. FILL OUT THE MISSING VERSES TO MATTHEW 22:11. USE YOUR MEMORY ONLY. (WE USED THE ESV TRANSLATION)

For many _____ _____, but few _____ _____.

WRITE OUT MATTHEW 22:11

_____

_____

_____

_____

_____

_____

_____

ANOTHER UNIQUE WAY TO MEMORIZE SCRIPTURE IS TO WRITE ONLY THE FIRST LETTER OF EACH WORD. TRY IT BELOW USING THIS PASSAGE. (SEPARATE) EACH LETTER WITH A COMMA)

_____

_____

_____

_____

Scripture Memorization

First we will Read the passage 10 times, and then say the passage aloud 10 times.

WITHOUT LOOKING IN YOUR BIBLE. FILL OUT THE MISSING VERSES TO JOHN 6:44. USE YOUR MEMORY ONLY. (WE USED THE ESV TRANSLATION)

No one can _____ ____ ____ unless the Father who _____ ____ draws him. And ___ _____ _____ him up on the _____ day.

WRITE OUT JOHN 6:44

_____

_____

_____

_____

_____

_____

_____

ANOTHER UNIQUE WAY TO MEMORIZE SCRIPTURE IS TO WRITE ONLY THE FIRST LETTER OF EACH WORD. TRY IT BELOW USING THIS PASSAGE. (SEPARATE) EACH LETTER WITH A COMMA)

_____

_____

_____

_____

First we will Read the passage 10 times, and then say the passage aloud 10 times.

WITHOUT LOOKING IN YOUR BIBLE. FILL OUT THE MISSING VERSES TO ECCLESIASTES 7:20. USE YOUR MEMORY ONLY. (WE USED THE ESV TRANSLATION)

Surely _____ _____ ____ a righteous man on _____ who does good and _____ _____.

WRITE OUT ECCLESIASTES 7:20

_____

_____

_____

_____

_____

_____

ANOTHER UNIQUE WAY TO MEMORIZE SCRIPTURE IS TO WRITE ONLY THE FIRST LETTER OF EACH WORD. TRY IT BELOW USING THIS PASSAGE. (SEPARATE) EACH LETTER WITH A COMMA)

_____

_____

_____

_____

First we will Read the passage 10 times, and then say the passage aloud 10 times.

WITHOUT LOOKING IN YOUR BIBLE. FILL OUT THE MISSING VERSES TO JOHN 14:17. USE YOUR MEMORY ONLY. (WE USED THE ESV TRANSLATION)

Even the _____ ____ _____, whom the world cannot _____, because it neither _____ _____ nor _____ _____. You know him, for ____ _____ with you and will ____ ____ you.

WRITE OUT JOHN 14:17

_____

_____

_____

_____

_____

_____

_____

ANOTHER UNIQUE WAY TO MEMORIZE SCRIPTURE IS TO WRITE ONLY THE FIRST LETTER OF EACH WORD. TRY IT BELOW USING THIS PASSAGE. (SEPARATE) EACH LETTER WITH A COMMA)

_____

_____

_____

_____

First we will Read the passage 10 times, and then say the passage aloud 10 times.

WITHOUT LOOKING IN YOUR BIBLE. FILL OUT THE MISSING VERSES TO PSALM 90:2. USE YOUR MEMORY ONLY. (WE USED THE ESV TRANSLATION)

Before _____ _____ were brought forth, or ever you _____ _____ the earth and _____ _____, from everlasting to everlasting _____ _____ God.

WRITE OUT PSALM 90:2

_____

_____

_____

_____

_____

_____

_____

ANOTHER UNIQUE WAY TO MEMORIZE SCRIPTURE IS TO WRITE ONLY THE FIRST LETTER OF EACH WORD. TRY IT BELOW USING THIS PASSAGE. (SEPARATE) EACH LETTER WITH A COMMA)

_____

_____

_____

_____

First we will Read the passage 10 times, and then say the passage aloud 10 times.

WITHOUT LOOKING IN YOUR BIBLE. FILL OUT THE MISSING VERSES TO PSALM 145:17. USE YOUR MEMORY ONLY. (WE USED THE ESV TRANSLATION)

The Lord ____ _____ *in all* _____ _____ *and kind in all his* _____.

WRITE OUT PSALM 145:17

_____

_____

_____

_____

_____

_____

_____

ANOTHER UNIQUE WAY TO MEMORIZE SCRIPTURE IS TO WRITE ONLY THE FIRST LETTER OF EACH WORD. TRY IT BELOW USING THIS PASSAGE. (SEPARATE) EACH LETTER WITH A COMMA)

_____

_____

_____

_____

First we will Read the passage 10 times, and then say the passage aloud 10 times.

WITHOUT LOOKING IN YOUR BIBLE, FILL OUT THE MISSING VERSES TO 1 THESSALONIANS 5:23-24. USE YOUR MEMORY ONLY. (WE USED THE ESV TRANSLATION)

Now _____ _____ God of peace himself _____ _____ completely, and may your whole _____ _____ _____ and body be kept _____ at the coming of _____ Jesus Christ. He who _____ you is _____; he will _____ do it.

WRITE OUT 1 THESSALONIANS 5:23-24

_____

_____

_____

_____

_____

_____

ANOTHER UNIQUE WAY TO MEMORIZE SCRIPTURE IS TO WRITE ONLY THE FIRST LETTER OF EACH WORD. TRY IT BELOW USING THIS PASSAGE. (SEPARATE) EACH LETTER WITH A COMMA)

_____

_____

_____

_____

Scripture Memorization

First we will Read the passage 10 times, and then say the passage aloud 10 times.

WITHOUT LOOKING IN YOUR BIBLE. FILL OUT THE MISSING VERSES TO JOHN 17:1-2. USE YOUR MEMORY ONLY. (WE USED THE ESV TRANSLATION)

When Jesus _____ _____ these words, he _____ _____ his eyes to heaven, and said, "_____, the hour has _____; glorify your Son that _____ _____ may _____ you, since you have _____ _____ authority over _____ _____, to give _____ life to all whom you _____ _____ him.

WRITE OUT JOHN 17:1-2

_____

_____

_____

_____

_____

_____

_____

ANOTHER UNIQUE WAY TO MEMORIZE SCRIPTURE IS TO WRITE ONLY THE FIRST LETTER OF EACH WORD. TRY IT BELOW USING THIS PASSAGE. (SEPARATE) EACH LETTER WITH A COMMA)

_____

_____

_____

_____

First we will Read the passage 10 times, and then say the passage aloud 10 times.

WITHOUT LOOKING IN YOUR BIBLE. FILL OUT THE MISSING VERSES TO JOHN 3:5-7. USE YOUR MEMORY ONLY. (WE USED THE ESV TRANSLATION)

_____ answered, "Truly, truly, I say to you, unless _____ ____ _____ of _____ and the _____, he cannot enter _____ _____ of God. That which is born of the _____ ____ _____, and that which is _____ of the _____ is spirit. Do not _____ that I said to you, 'You must ____ _____ again.'

WRITE OUT JOHN 3:5-7

_____

_____

_____

_____

_____

_____

ANOTHER UNIQUE WAY TO MEMORIZE SCRIPTURE IS TO WRITE ONLY THE FIRST LETTER OF EACH WORD. TRY IT BELOW USING THIS PASSAGE. (SEPARATE) EACH LETTER WITH A COMMA)

_____

_____

_____

_____

Scripture Memorization

First we will Read the passage 10 times, and then say the passage aloud 10 times.

WITHOUT LOOKING IN YOUR BIBLE, FILL OUT THE MISSING VERSES TO ROMANS 8:7-8. USE YOUR MEMORY ONLY. (WE USED THE ESV TRANSLATION)

The mind _____ ____ the flesh is _____ to God; it does not _____ to God's law, _____ _____ ____ do so. Those who are in the _____ ____ _____ _____ cannot please God.

WRITE OUT ROMANS 8:7-8

_____

_____

_____

_____

_____

_____

ANOTHER UNIQUE WAY TO MEMORIZE SCRIPTURE IS TO WRITE ONLY THE FIRST LETTER OF EACH WORD. TRY IT BELOW USING THIS PASSAGE. (SEPARATE) EACH LETTER WITH A COMMA)

_____

_____

_____

_____

First we will Read the passage 10 times, and then say the passage aloud 10 times.

WITHOUT LOOKING IN YOUR BIBLE. FILL OUT THE MISSING VERSES TO 2 TIMOTHY 2:25-26. USE YOUR MEMORY ONLY. (WE USED THE ESV TRANSLATION)

Correcting his _____ with _____. God may perhaps grant them _____ leading to a _____ of the _____, and _____ may come to their _____ and _____ from the _____ of the devil, after _____ _____ by him to do _____ _____.

WRITE OUT 2 TIMOTHY 2:25-26

_____

_____

_____

_____

_____

_____

ANOTHER UNIQUE WAY TO MEMORIZE SCRIPTURE IS TO WRITE ONLY THE FIRST LETTER OF EACH WORD. TRY IT BELOW USING THIS PASSAGE. (SEPARATE) EACH LETTER WITH A COMMA)

_____

_____

_____

_____

Scripture Memorization

First we will Read the passage 10 times, and then say the passage aloud 10 times.

WITHOUT LOOKING IN YOUR BIBLE. FILL OUT THE MISSING VERSES TO 2 TIMOTHY 4:2. USE YOUR MEMORY ONLY. (WE USED THE ESV TRANSLATION)

_____ _____ _____; *be ready in season and* _____ ____ *season; reprove,* _____, *and* _____, *with complete patience and* _____.

WRITE OUT 2 TIMOTHY 4:2

_____

_____

_____

_____

_____

_____

ANOTHER UNIQUE WAY TO MEMORIZE SCRIPTURE IS TO WRITE ONLY THE FIRST LETTER OF EACH WORD. TRY IT BELOW USING THIS PASSAGE. (SEPARATE) EACH LETTER WITH A COMMA)

_____

_____

_____

_____

First we will Read the passage 10 times, and then say the passage aloud 10 times.

WITHOUT LOOKING IN YOUR BIBLE. FILL OUT THE MISSING VERSES TO ROMANS 5:18-19. USE YOUR MEMORY ONLY. (WE USED THE ESV TRANSLATION)

Therefore, as _____ _____ led to condemnation for _____ _____, so one act of _____ leads to _____ and _____ for all men. For ____ ____ the one man's _____ the many were made _____, so by the one man's _____, the many will be _____ _____.

WRITE OUT ROMANS 5:18-19

_____

_____

_____

_____

_____

_____

ANOTHER UNIQUE WAY TO MEMORIZE SCRIPTURE IS TO WRITE ONLY THE FIRST LETTER OF EACH WORD. TRY IT BELOW USING THIS PASSAGE. (SEPARATE) EACH LETTER WITH A COMMA)

_____

_____

_____

_____

Scripture Memorization

First we will Read the passage 10 times, and then say the passage aloud 10 times.

WITHOUT LOOKING IN YOUR BIBLE. FILL OUT THE MISSING VERSES TO EPHESIANS 1:4-6. USE YOUR MEMORY ONLY. (WE USED THE ESV TRANSLATION)

Even as he _____ ____ in him _____ _____ _____ of the world, that we should be _____ and _____ before him. In love he _____ us for _____ as sons through Jesus _____, according to the _____ of _____ _____, to the praise of his _____ _____, with which ____ _____ _____ us in the _____.

WRITE OUT EPHESIANS 1:4-6

_____

_____

_____

_____

_____

_____

_____

ANOTHER UNIQUE WAY TO MEMORIZE SCRIPTURE IS TO WRITE ONLY THE FIRST LETTER OF EACH WORD. TRY IT BELOW USING THIS PASSAGE. (SEPARATE) EACH LETTER WITH A COMMA)

_____

_____

_____

_____

Scripture Memorization

First we will Read the passage 10 times, and then say the passage aloud 10 times.

WITHOUT LOOKING IN YOUR BIBLE. FILL OUT THE MISSING VERSES TO PSALM 51:12. USE YOUR MEMORY ONLY. (WE USED THE ESV TRANSLATION)

_____ to me the _____ of your _____, and uphold me with a _____ _____.

WRITE OUT PSALM 51:12

_____

_____

_____

_____

_____

_____

_____

ANOTHER UNIQUE WAY TO MEMORIZE SCRIPTURE IS TO WRITE ONLY THE FIRST LETTER OF EACH WORD. TRY IT BELOW USING THIS PASSAGE. (SEPARATE) EACH LETTER WITH A COMMA)

_____

_____

_____

_____

First we will Read the passage 10 times, and then say the passage aloud 10 times.

WITHOUT LOOKING IN YOUR BIBLE. FILL OUT THE MISSING VERSES TO PSALM 37:28. USE YOUR MEMORY ONLY. (WE USED THE ESV TRANSLATION)

For the Lord _____ _____; he will not _____ his _____. They are _____ _____, but the children of the _____ shall be _____ off.

WRITE OUT PSALM 37:28

_____

_____

_____

_____

_____

_____

_____

ANOTHER UNIQUE WAY TO MEMORIZE SCRIPTURE IS TO WRITE ONLY THE FIRST LETTER OF EACH WORD. TRY IT BELOW USING THIS PASSAGE. (SEPARATE) EACH LETTER WITH A COMMA)

_____

_____

_____

_____

First we will Read the passage 10 times, and then say the passage aloud 10 times.

WITHOUT LOOKING IN YOUR BIBLE. FILL OUT THE MISSING VERSES TO ROMANS 9:21. USE YOUR MEMORY ONLY. (WE USED THE ESV TRANSLATION)

Has the _____ no right over _____ _____, to make out of the same lump _____ _____ for _____ use and another for _____ use?

WRITE OUT ROMANS 9:21

_____

_____

_____

_____

_____

_____

_____

ANOTHER UNIQUE WAY TO MEMORIZE SCRIPTURE IS TO WRITE ONLY THE FIRST LETTER OF EACH WORD. TRY IT BELOW USING THIS PASSAGE. (SEPARATE) EACH LETTER WITH A COMMA)

_____

_____

_____

_____

Scripture Memorization

First we will Read the passage 10 times, and then say the passage aloud 10 times.

WITHOUT LOOKING IN YOUR BIBLE. FILL OUT THE MISSING VERSES TO
PROVERBS 21:1. USE YOUR MEMORY ONLY. (WE USED THE ESV
TRANSLATION)

*The king's _____ is a _____ ____ _____ in the hand of the
_____; he turns it _____ he will.*

WRITE OUT PROVERBS 21:1

_____

_____

_____

_____

_____

_____

_____

ANOTHER UNIQUE WAY TO MEMORIZE SCRIPTURE IS TO WRITE ONLY
THE FIRST LETTER OF EACH WORD. TRY IT BELOW USING THIS
PASSAGE. (SEPARATE) EACH LETTER WITH A COMMA)

_____

_____

_____

_____

Scripture Memorization

First we will Read the passage 10 times, and then say the passage aloud 10 times.

WITHOUT LOOKING IN YOUR BIBLE. FILL OUT THE MISSING VERSES TO 2 THESSALONIANS 2:14. USE YOUR MEMORY ONLY. (WE USED THE ESV TRANSLATION)

To this he _____ _____ through our _____, so that you may obtain ___ _____ of our Lord _____ Christ.

WRITE OUT 2 THESSALONIANS 2:14

_____
_____
_____
_____
_____
_____
_____

ANOTHER UNIQUE WAY TO MEMORIZE SCRIPTURE IS TO WRITE ONLY THE FIRST LETTER OF EACH WORD. TRY IT BELOW USING THIS PASSAGE. (SEPARATE) EACH LETTER WITH A COMMA)

_____
_____
_____
_____

First we will Read the passage 10 times, and then say the passage aloud 10 times.

WITHOUT LOOKING IN YOUR BIBLE. FILL OUT THE MISSING VERSES TO DEUTERONOMY 29:29. USE YOUR MEMORY ONLY. (WE USED THE ESV TRANSLATION)

The _____ _____ belong to the Lord our God, but the _____ that are _____ belong to us and to our children _____, that we may do all the _____ of this _____.

WRITE OUT DEUTERONOMY 29:29

_____

_____

_____

_____

_____

_____

_____

ANOTHER UNIQUE WAY TO MEMORIZE SCRIPTURE IS TO WRITE ONLY THE FIRST LETTER OF EACH WORD. TRY IT BELOW USING THIS PASSAGE. (SEPARATE) EACH LETTER WITH A COMMA)

_____

_____

_____

_____

First we will Read the passage 10 times, and then say the passage aloud 10 times.

WITHOUT LOOKING IN YOUR BIBLE. FILL OUT THE MISSING VERSES TO JEREMIAH 17:9. USE YOUR MEMORY ONLY. (WE USED THE ESV TRANSLATION)

The _____ is _____ above _____ things, and _____ sick; who can _____ it?

WRITE OUT JEREMIAH 17:9

_____

_____

_____

_____

_____

_____

_____

ANOTHER UNIQUE WAY TO MEMORIZE SCRIPTURE IS TO WRITE ONLY THE FIRST LETTER OF EACH WORD. TRY IT BELOW USING THIS PASSAGE. (SEPARATE) EACH LETTER WITH A COMMA)

_____

_____

_____

_____

First we will Read the passage 10 times, and then say the passage aloud 10 times.

WITHOUT LOOKING IN YOUR BIBLE. FILL OUT THE MISSING VERSES TO HEBREWS 12:3. USE YOUR MEMORY ONLY. (WE USED THE ESV TRANSLATION)

_____ *him who* _____ *from sinners such* _____ _____ *himself, so that* _____ _____ _____ *grow* _____ *or fainthearted.*

WRITE OUT HEBREWS 12:3

_____

_____

_____

_____

_____

_____

_____

ANOTHER UNIQUE WAY TO MEMORIZE SCRIPTURE IS TO WRITE ONLY THE FIRST LETTER OF EACH WORD. TRY IT BELOW USING THIS PASSAGE. (SEPARATE) EACH LETTER WITH A COMMA)

_____

_____

_____

_____

First we will Read the passage 10 times, and then say the passage aloud 10 times.

WITHOUT LOOKING IN YOUR BIBLE. FILL OUT THE MISSING VERSES TO ISAIAH 46:9-10. USE YOUR MEMORY ONLY. (WE USED THE ESV TRANSLATION)

Remember the _____ _____ of old; for ___ ____ _____, and there is no _____; I am God, and there is _____ like me, _____ the end from the _____ and from _____ _____ things not yet done, saying, 'My _____ shall stand, and I will _____ all my _____.'

WRITE OUT ISAIAH 46:9-10

_____

_____

_____

_____

_____

_____

ANOTHER UNIQUE WAY TO MEMORIZE SCRIPTURE IS TO WRITE ONLY THE FIRST LETTER OF EACH WORD. TRY IT BELOW USING THIS PASSAGE. (SEPARATE) EACH LETTER WITH A COMMA)

_____

_____

_____

_____

Recommended Resources

WEBSITES

www.thegospelcoalition.org
www.thebiblicallysoundwoman.com
www.ligonier.org
www.sheshallbecalled.com
www.wholemagazine.org
www.narrowmindedwoman.com
www.shereadstruth.com
www.jenthorn.com
www.theothoughts.com
www.fishwithtrish.com
www.reasonabletheology.com
www.truthforlife.org
www.unlockingthebible.org
www.kristenwetherell.com
www.desiringgod.org
www.naomistable.com
www.monergism.com
www.biblethinkingwoman.com
www.laradentremont.com
www.reviveourhearts.com
www.jasminelholmes.com
www.jenwilkin.net
jenwilkin.podbean.com
www.unpopularthemovie.com
www.wellwateredwomen.com
www.challies.com
www.logos.com

BOOKS

Women of the Word by Jen Wilkin
Knowing God by J.I. Packer
Attributes of God by A.W. Pink
None Like Him by Jen Wilkin
Adorned by Nancy Leigh DeMoss
Lies Women Believe by Nancy Leigh DeMoss
When People Are Big and God Is Small by Ed Welch
Humble Roots by Hannah Anderson
Trusting God by Jerry Bridges
Respectable Sins by Jerry Bridges
Basic Bible Interpretation by Roy B. Zuck
Toward An Exegetical Theology by Walter C. Kaiser, Jr.
Sing a New Song by Lydia Brownback
The Secret Thoughts of an Unlikely Convert by Rosaria Butterfield
Systematic Theology by Wayne Grudem
Biblical Doctrine by John MacArthur
Passion and Purity by Elisabeth Elliot

PODCASTS

She Proves Faithful
The Biblically Sound Woman
She Shall Be Called
Truth's Table
Doctrine and Devotion
Equipping Eve
Risen Motherhood
Journey Women
Women's Hope Project
Following Christ
Knowing Faith
Look at the Book
Renewing Your Mind
Revive Our Hearts
Theology Refresh
Truth For Life
The Briefing
Grace to You Radio
Ask Pastor John
Mortification of Sin
When We Understand the Text
Mia Davies (God-Centered Success)

About the Author

Jennifer Lucy Tyler *is an entrepreneur, author, speaker, missionary, and Bible teacher. She is passionate about teaching women how to live missional within their communities; sharing the love of Christ from the four corners of their block to the four corners of the world. She is the founder of Soul Circles, a girl's night out event where women learn basic principles to studying the Bible. Her husband, Jeffrey Tyler serves as the Connections Pastor at New Life Church in LaPlata, MD. They both enjoy serving their local church, loving on their community, watching Marvel and DC Comic movies, trying new restaurants, and traveling around the world. They reside in White Plains, MD with their dog Shadow.*

Instagram: @mrslucytyler Facebook: JenniferLucyTyler

Made in the USA
Columbia, SC
16 February 2019